Love,
Mark, Becky, Justin, Shirley Anne,
Jaylee, + Dara

TO:

_____

FROM:

_____

DATE:

_____

HOOKED for LIFE

by JIMMY HOUSTON

COUNTRYMAN

HOOKED *for* LIFE

by Jimmy Houston

Copyright © 1999 by Jimmy Houston. Published by J. Countryman,
a division of Thomas Nelson, Inc. Nashville, Tennessee 37214

Project Editor: Pat Matuszak

Special thanks to Dr. Andy Bowman, scriptural contributor

Unless otherwise indicated, all Scripture quotations in this book
are from the New King James Version of the Bible (NKJV),
copyright © 1979, 1980, 1982, by Thomas Nelson, Publishers, Inc.
and are used by permission.

Designed by Koechel Peterson & Associates,
Minneapolis, Minnesota

Photography credits:
Koechel Peterson & Associates — Endpapers, 1, 6, 7, 8-9, 10, 12, 19,
22-23, 24, 26, 30, 33, 36-37, 39, 41, 42, 45, 49, 51, 52-53, 54, 56, 59,
61, 64, 66-67, 71, 73, 74-75, 76, 78, 81, 84, 88-89, 91, 94, 96, 101,
102-103, 107, 111, 113, 115, 116, 118-119, 121, 127
Jim Linder — 2-3, 21, 46-47, 68, 83, 92, 98-99, 105, 109, 123

ISBN: 08499-5504-1

Printed and bound in Belgium

TABLE OF CONTENTS

FOREWORD

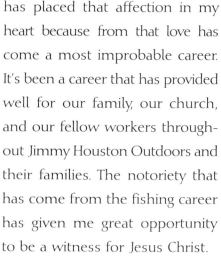

At a very early age, I came to love the sport of fishing. I can't remember my first fish or my first fishing trip. I'm sure it was with my dad or granddad, probably both. As the years have gone by, my love for fishing has grown deeper. I praise God that He has placed that affection in my heart because from that love has come a most improbable career. It's been a career that has provided well for our family, our church, and our fellow workers throughout Jimmy Houston Outdoors and their families. The notoriety that has come from the fishing career has given me great opportunity to be a witness for Jesus Christ.

Also, at a very early age, I made a decision that Jesus Christ would be the Lord and Savior of my life. That commitment was the most important decision I've ever made. Without that decision and commitment, I truly believe that all the other things would never have come to be. With that decision came the beginning of a walk with God that has grown closer as the years have gone by.

Do I live as close to God as He wants me to? Of course not! But, I've been drawn nearer to God, and my prayer is to follow Him more closely each day. Since that decision, God has orchestrated my life in a manner that is beyond my wildest imagination.

As you read this book, keep in mind that God is the Master Builder. All the events of life are intended to train and teach us more of God's grace and love. He wants us to follow after His desires: the things that will make us more like Him. We may each find a different pond to fish at, but in the end, God wants to bring every one of us into closer union with Him. He teaches us through every experience from our youth up.

Jimmy Houston,
June 1999

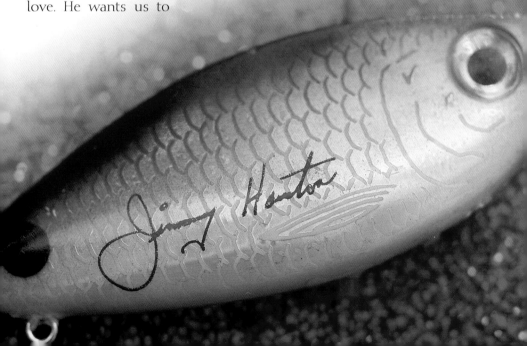

PART ONE

A Life
of Fishing

Isn't it just like God to use such seemingly insignificant events as catching crawdads to prepare us for greater challenges in life? The Scripture says, "Whatever your hand finds to do, do it with your might." Put your mind, heart, and body into whatever task you attempt. Not just for the event at hand, but as a great training ground for the rest of your life.

MY FIRST SPAWNING BASS

Tribulation produces perseverance;
and perseverance, character.

- ROMANS 5:3–4

I encountered my first "spawning bass" in a backwater pond. I can still see that big ole pot-bellied bass laying under that giant willow limb. It was the biggest bass I'd ever seen. I couldn't figure out why she always stayed in the same spot but wouldn't bite anything. Every lure in my limited tackle box was tried unsuccessfully. Finally, I crawled out on that willow tree limb directly over that bass and dangled a live minnow in the fish's face. That bass probably didn't weigh over five or six pounds, but when I took it to my grandma's to have her help me clean it, you'd have thought I had just caught the world record.

Like catching that spawning bass, life takes a lot of patience, perseverance, and the willingness to adapt in order to succeed. Most of us want whatever we are trying to accomplish to happen right now. But as we grow in God and grow older, we usually also grow in patience. Some folks pray, "God give me patience, and I want it right now!"

I never used to pray for patience for fear God would grant it to me. God has finally taught me that patience is indeed a virtue; and sure enough He is doling it out to me in amounts I can handle. Ask God for patience. It will improve your relationship with others and make your life happier and less stressful. Praise God that He is patient with us.

PRAYER

Lord, I am just so grateful for Your patience with me. Help me to remember how You've given grace to me and help me to be like You — patient with others.

THE FAMILY—A GIFT FROM GOD

Therefore a man will leave his father and mother and be joined to his wife, and they shall become one flesh.

-GENESIS 2:24

One of the many blessings God ordained for me when I accepted Jesus as my Lord at twelve years of age was a wonderful and beautiful wife. Never mind that we lived south of Oklahoma City and she was a nine-year-old Cherokee Indian girl who lived on a creek bank some two hundred miles away. I'll always believe that on that Sunday morning at Crestline Baptist Church, God looked around and said: "These two oughta' work out fine."

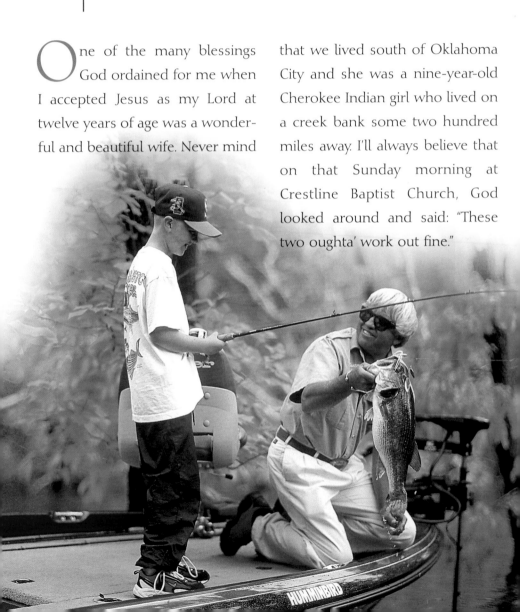

After thirty-five years of marriage, I still remember the first day I saw her. She was walking in the creek in her swimsuit, soaking wet, with long, black wet hair. She probably looked pretty scraggly at the time, but as I look back, the memory is beautiful. I guess God checked that off His worksheet for my life that day.

Our marriage has had its rough spots—mostly my fault—but God has given us a heart to love and forgive. These trying times, as difficult as they are, have actually grown our relationship and love for each other. God also gave us a daughter, Sherri, and a son, Jamie, and another child, Richard, whom we've raised since he was three weeks old.

Our family unit is not only a loving family but a working family. We started our kids working in the business when they were eight or nine years old. We gave them jobs with responsibility, and they were able to learn what it takes to be successful. We included them in everything we did from work to fishing tournaments—we still do. And we took our kids to church. You can't give your kids any greater gift than to raise them in church. I guess the bottom line is relationships—intimate and personal and lasting. A family—what a great gift from God!

PRAYER

Thank You dear Lord for giving us the privilege of having wonderful families, for teaching us that a family binds us to You in a loving way.

THE JOY OF FISHING

Jesus said, "These things I have spoken to you, that My joy may remain in you, and that your joy may be full."

-JOHN 15:11

Without a doubt, fishing is fun. What a sport! You need no great skills or talents to have fun fishing. You don't have to be tall or strong or fast or particularly coordinated. And you can have fun at age four or one hundred and four.

Most of my early fishing trips were with my dad and my two uncles—Uncle John and Uncle Gene. These weren't bass fishing

trips very often. They were mostly catfish or crappie. One of my favorite places to fish was the Washita River, south of Purcell, Oklahoma. In the hot summer the river would get really low, in fact, dry in most places, leaving small potholes of water below huge log-jams. We'd walk from hole to hole, sometimes ending up miles from the car.

I can still see Uncle John precariously perched on the end of a log with rod and reel in hand. Envision a great blue heron perched at attention on that log waiting for a shad and you can "see" Uncle John waiting for a catfish to strike.

Even as a young boy, I saw God's work while fishing up and down a river. No matter how much rain or how little, those catfish always survived in that river. The washed-out areas and potholes always held just enough water for the fish to get by in even the hottest and driest summer. As those catfish are important to God, so are we important to Him. He'll never let us run out of water no matter how tough times are. I don't suppose those catfish ever worry about that river drying up. That's called faith, and it's the basis for everything we will ever be.

Lord, You have given us wonderful times in our life while fishing. We ask You now to lead us in the ways You would have us walk so that the fulfillment of happiness and joy are present.

THE REWARDS OF FISHING

Lay up for yourselves treasures in heaven,
where neither moth nor rust destroys.
—MATTHEW 6:20

Fishing is simply a game of rewards whether you're fishing with your son or daughter or competing in the Bassmaster's Classic. You expect something positive or rewarding to happen on every trip. Reporters have asked about my most rewarding fishing trips. Without a doubt, a trip with my kids or my wife or my dad comes to mind. As rewarding financially and career-wise as a tournament win or angler-of-the-year title is, they pale in comparison to the rewards of real-life experiences with those you love most.

When Sherri was twelve or thirteen we were filming a show in Texas. Sherri hooked, fought, and landed a huge seven-pound bass on a white spinnerbait. Her excitement and thrill, and mine, reached unbelievable heights. That happened over twenty years ago, and I can still see that episode play in my mind just like it happened yesterday.

When Jamie graduated from high school, I took him to Venezuela for five days of peacock bassing and one day catching white marlin in saltwater. Our boat was boarded by the authorities on our saltwater day and impounded by machine-gun-toting police, but we were allowed to take our fishing gear and go ashore. How could I ever put a price tag on a father/son trip like that?

And Chris and I have had literally hundreds of days that are individually unique. We haven't caught a lot of fish every time, but each day has had its own life. One of the best ever was on our home lake, Lake Tenkiller, on a hot July night. We were catfishing with Pole Cracker, a flavor of Catfish Charlie's stink baits. We were anchored on a flat in twenty feet of water near Six-Shooter Creek. We baited the area with 36 percent protein hog pellets (that's pig feed). The catfish love it and will swim for quite a ways for the pellets. We caught so many channel cats that night we ran out of bait and had to open up Mom and Dad's store to get more. When daylight came we had 153 catfish!

Long after the tournament winnings are spent and dust is gathering on the trophies, unique memories like these are the rewards in fishing. Jesus said to store up rewards in heaven; rewards that will lead to eternal life. Too often, we are guilty of pursuing worldly rewards. As we reflect back on our life—our fishing trips and our goals—we can see what the important rewards really are. Very seldom do we see worldly goods or accomplishments.

PRAYER

What a reward to go fishing, Lord, and have a bountiful catch. But the true joy is giving praise to You and knowing that Your love is ever-present.

THE DESIRE TO WIN

Yet in all things we are more than conquerors
through Him who loved us.

ROMANS 8:37

I believe the single greatest key to winning is knowing, without a doubt, that you have the ability to win. I've seen so many tournament fishermen struggle for years and then finally win a victory that changes their whole career—all of a sudden they begin to visit the winner's circle often. My friend Jim Bitter from Florida is a good example. Jim went for years without winning, but once he did win, he won often. Jim now knows he has the ability to win.

No matter how hard we struggle to win life's little "titles," we have been made for far more than that. Paul said in Romans, "We are more than conquerors through Him who loved us." The greatest victory of all is knowing Jesus as our personal Savior and living in the knowledge of His great love. To know Him and His pardon and to look forward to living with Him for eternity makes these other "wins" a little less demanding. We who know Christ are already winners. I wouldn't trade that for any or all of the titles and accolades this world can offer!

PRAYER

Dear God, we thank You for teaching us to win life's rewards, but we know the greatest reward is having a personal relationship with Your Son, Jesus Christ.

VICTORY THROUGH GOD'S WILL

But thanks be to God, who gives us the victory
through our Lord Jesus Christ.

-1 CORINTHIANS 15:57

My wife, Chris, has won every Bass'n Gal tournament ever held in the state of Tennessee. Three of those victories have come at Lake Chickamauga in Chattanooga. Two of the wins have been the coveted Bass'n Gal Classic. She speaks often of fish falling out of heaven, and that's pretty much what happened in her second Classic victory there.

Chris was near the top of the standings going into the final day but was having a miserable time catching bass. In fact, she had only two small keepers with less than thirty minutes of tournament time remaining. She was not going to win this tournament, but she made a run to the dam and hurriedly fished the rock rip-rap with a spinnerbait and a topwater. In those last desperate minutes she caught three nice bass, including one over three pounds, and miraculously won the tournament.

Did those fish just fall out of heaven? I could fill several books with stories just like this where God poured His blessings down on Chris and me. Do we live expecting these kinds of blessings? Yes we do. Even more incredible is the fact that God gives us blessings far greater than we can ever expect or hope for.

How can anyone expect such victory and blessings from God? I believe the key is seeking God's will in our lives.

To me, seeking and ultimately living in God's will is threefold: Prayer (about pretty much everything), reading the Bible (I do it daily), and being an active part of God's church. I really don't believe we can do these three things and stray too far from the will of God.

No, we won't be perfect, and yes, we'll mess up. But, if we're praying, reading God's Word, and being active in His church, His Holy Spirit will lead us out of trouble and keep us out of most bad situations.

Is God waiting to drop fish out of heaven? I think He is!

PRAYER

Thank You, Father, for tournament victories, for acclaimed success, and for giving us eternal hope in Jesus.

PART TWO

WHERE IS GOD LEADING ME?

God has a plan for all of us. It involves finding, knowing, and doing His will for our lives. Not everyone is expected or intended to fish for a living or preach or teach. We're all intended to find God's purpose, His plan, and get after it! We should expend every energy and everything we have on doing the best job He has called us to do.

LOOKING FOR PURPOSE

Therefore, whether you eat or drink, or whatever you do, do all to the glory of God.

-I CORINTHIANS 10:31

In my wildest imagination, I never dreamed of becoming a professional fisherman. When Chris and I first started fishing tournaments back in college, there was no such animal as a pro fisherman. We were fishing purely for the fun of it.

We're constantly asked how to become a pro fisherman. I believe anyone's first priority in life, regardless of what career they seek, is to establish a close, working relationship with Jesus. Without that, any career is going to be more difficult, and whatever success you have will not be very fulfilling. A lot of folks have success and then ask themselves, Is that all there is?

Second, I believe you need a good education. One of my parents' greatest accomplishments was to send me through college.

Keep in mind, college is not the only place you get an education. Every job, every trip and every conversation should be a learning process. Whatever you do, work as hard as you can at your education, no matter what age you are.

Third, of course, you must develop your fishing skills and abilities. Fishing takes physical skills and talents plus mental abilities. Read every book and article you can get your hands on and don't just read, study! Watch every television show and video. Go to every seminar. Take notes on everything. Fill your mind with knowledge about this sport.

Go fishing as much as you can, with as many different people as you can—you can always learn something important from everyone. Make it your goal to learn something every day, from the guy or gal in the other end of the boat. Fish as many tournaments as you can—first to learn and second to win. Remember, the pros fish 200 to 250 days per year.

You notice I haven't mentioned how to get sponsors, someone to pay your way. Don't worry about it. You develop what it takes and the sponsorships will come. As I said, we never planned on making fishing a career. God planned it for us. We're just keeping our spinnerbait wet.

PRAYER

Lord, let me go all out,
100 percent of the time doing Your will.
That's really success for me.

THE DAILY HOPE

This is the day the LORD has made;
we will rejoice and be glad in it.

-PSALM 118:24

One of the great things about fishing is you never really know what's going to happen when you head out each day. When we're filming for ESPN we never use a script or write a story line. We let each trip create its own story. There's always something that will make that day unique. We never stage or pre-catch a fish. The live action makes each day's show different from all the rest.

That's really what life is all about: taking each day God gives us and making it special. If we would start each day with a prayer of commitment to God, it would make every day special, and would draw us closer to Him.

Many times, our biggest losses and failures have turned into some of our greatest victories. One such instance happened with MonArk Boats, our aluminum boat sponsor. MonArk was owned by Brunswick Marine. Then MonArk was sold by Brunswick to Sylvan, and I had a little over a year left on my contract.

Sylvan didn't want me so Brunswick offered to buy out my contract. I agreed but, in essence, I had just been fired. It was a big loss, but I knew God was in control. Within days, my longtime friend Johnny Morris called and asked me to go to work for Tracker Aluminum and Bass Pro Shops. We were also in the catalog business, and Johnny agreed to buy our catalog and all our inventory. In addition, I got to fish out of a much better aluminum boat!

So, don't get too concerned when things don't work out just as you planned. When you place God first, He will always have a better plan for your life. It might not happen right away, but rest assured, His plan is best.

PRAYER

Lord, thank You for today. I know You gave it to me to celebrate and anticipate. Help me to be grateful and to experience Your best for me.

A DIFFERENT DAY EVERY DAY

*We, who with unveiled faces all reflect the Lord's glory,
are being transformed into His likeness.*

-2 CORINTHIANS 3:18 NIV

You learn very early in a tournament fishing career that no two days are alike. It's highly unusual to fish a three-day tournament and have success doing the same thing in the same places. To score high in the tournament, you must have the ability to adapt not only on a daily basis, but often several times during the day. This is probably the single most difficult thing for a tournament fisherman. It's especially difficult if you have done well the first couple of days in a tournament and then must make a severe change the final day. The secret to making these changes successfully is to have the *courage* to make them.

We held the Brunswick Fins Game at Disneyworld in Orlando, Florida for several years. This tournament is patterned after the Skins game in golf. The lake is divided into six holes. Each hole is fished for fifty minutes by all contestants and money can be won on each hole. Pounds are converted into points, which makes a tie a real possibility. In case of a tie, the money is carried on to the next hole. The final hole is worth $30,000. The players were Roland Martin, Hank Parker, Gary Klein, Shaw Grigsby, and myself.

One year the fish were pretty much being caught on plastic worms and Hot Spots, away from the bank on drops and ditches. Hank and Roland had tied the fifth hole, which was worth $15,000. That money carried over, making the last hole worth $45,000. I had won the first two holes totaling $7,500 but had really bombed out on holes three, four, and five.

On the last hole, it clouded up and the wind started blowing. I left the open water and went to the bank, working a shad colored Pop-R. Almost immediately, I hooked and lost a three-pounder and a five-pounder. I did follow these up with four nice bass (one over four pounds) and won the hole and the $45,000. Ironically, no other competitor moved to shallow water.

Life also presents no two days that are alike. Each day brings about its own challenges, its own victories, its own defeats. In order to make each day successful, we must be able to adapt to people and situations. Our reliance on God's Word and our desire to live a life pleasing to Him will allow us to thrive in any situation. It will also give us the tools to get along and work with anyone.

Have the courage to change in tournament competition and have the faith to rely on God as each day brings about new challenges in your life.

PRAYER
There is wonderment, Lord, in how You make each day a blessing—a day of strengthening.

TOMORROW'S REWARDS

Bless the LORD, O my soul, and forget not all His benefits.

-PSALM 103:2

Tournament success is ultimately keyed to practice success. Tomorrow's rewards in tournament competition means learning and using the right techniques in practice. Most tournament fishermen work hard during competition, but that number dwindles during the practice rounds. Two of the hardest working practicers I know are Roland Martin and George Cochran. Their trucks and trailers are always some of the last at the ramp during practice days.

My personal idea about practice days is to use them to catch up with the rest of the field. I don't pre-fish tournaments, so when official practice starts I'm generally behind in knowledge of the lake and where the fish are located. Competitors that are quitting at three or four o'clock in the after-

noon are actually giving me a few extra hours each day to learn more. Simply put, go early and stay late!

Additionally, you must practice smart. I practice with my wife, Chris. She's actually another mind in the boat and has an uncanny ability to figure out bass behavior. In addition, Chris and I always throw different lures and try different techniques. We actually do double time during practice days.

In making decisions during practice rounds, always consider the type of water you're fishing, what that water is doing at the time, the weather, and the time of the year. These four criteria let you figure out the tournament water.

As we walk with God, each day also brings hope for tomorrow's rewards—just like practice days in fishing tournaments. The biggest reward that God promises is eternal life. This is what Jesus came to accomplish—eternal life for God's children. God also promises rewards on a daily basis for His people.

The Psalmist wrote, "Bless the LORD O my soul, and forget not all His benefits." He was saying that we should worship and honor God with our true selves and remember the blessings He shares with us. God asks His children to trust Him and try Him to see the blessings He will shower upon us. Let's be careful to look for them and to enjoy not just the gift, but the Giver.

PRAYER

Lord, help me to live today with an eye open for chances to improve my life, knowing You've given me more than I deserve. May I honor You with all that I am.

LEARNING DAILY

So teach us to number our days,
That we may gain a heart of wisdom.

-PSALMS 90:12

When you know all there is to know about fishing and tournaments it's time to throw away your rods and put your Trilene line on your weed-trimmer. The truth is, fishing is a continual, daily, learning process. As you watch tournament years unfold, you'll see fishermen have "hot" years and dominate the tour only to fall back in the pack. The BASS-Angler-of-the-Year title is a great example. Many have won, but few have won more than once. Is a person less skillful or talented if he places lower in the standings? Of course not, part of the problem is the other competitors have caught up.

The learning process at the professional tournament level is like a game of leap frog: the pros continually leap over each other in knowledge and skills. The beautiful part of this game is that we're always helping and teaching each other. Most of what we learn, we learn from those we are competing against.

A personal walk and relationship with God is also a daily learning experience. The Bible says we are babes in Christ when we're saved, no matter what age we are. From that baby status we grow as Christians, and the growth enriches our lives.

Thankfully, we don't have to tackle this growth on our own. When we are saved, God indwells us with His Holy Spirit. His Spirit leads us in everything we do. He guides us as we study God's Word. He nurtures the love we have for our families and fellow Christians. He creates in us the ability to become the kind of person God wants us to be. And the Holy Spirit leads us as we pray. When we pray, God listens, and when God answers, we learn.

PRAYER

Lord, let me learn daily what I must do to live today to its fullest and let tomorrow take care of itself.

KNOWING MY LIMITS

He must manage his own family well and see that
his children obey him with proper respect.

-1 TIMOTHY 3:4 NIV

Catching the full limit of bass is the goal of every tournament fisherman. In some tournaments you're confident a limit will come quickly and easily. Others, you're still confident of a limit, but know it will be difficult to come by.

One of the limits we all work under is time. Our tournament day will always run out of time whether we're ready to go to the weigh-in or not.

Our time on this earth is allotted also. The Bible says our days are numbered. The difference is that we're not told in advance when we'll be weighed in! Many of us live to a ripe old age, but the important thing is what we do with our allotted time.

I keep a horrendous schedule, doing fifty-two television shows and making over eighty personal appearances while working with sponsors and fishing tournaments. This keeps me on the road a great deal—in fact almost all the time. But I have a statement written on the top of the page of every month of my calendar. "I have all the time I need to do all God intends me to do this year!" This puts God at the head of all my scheduling.

I truly believe that our biggest time allocations must be to our family. Even with extremely busy schedules, our family has always spent a tremendous amount of time together. We schedule almost everything we do with family involvement planned into it. We've done this since Day One of our marriage, and it has continued through our kids, their marriages, and onto the grandkids. God made the family and designed the family as the centerpiece of creation. No matter how difficult it may be, work hard to involve your family in everything you do. I'm confident this is God's plan.

PRAYER

Father God, we've been given limits in our lives. But we know that You have given us what is best for our lives, day by day.

PART THREE

THE BASICS
of
FISHING

I always thank God for every day, even the most difficult and trying ones. I always thank God for every fish I catch, even if it's still last place in a tournament or not enough to make a television show. I thank God for the days when I don't even catch a single fish. After all, every single thing we have or do is a blessing from God.

MY TEACHER

Six days do your work, but on the seventh day do not work.

- EXODUS 23:12 NIV

My teacher throughout my life was my dad, Jack Houston. One of the most valuable things I learned from Dad early on was the value of hard work. Dad drove a taxicab and then became a cookie salesman for L. D. Jones Food Company. He drove a cookie truck and sold and delivered cookies. I rode the route with him a lot on Saturdays and during the summer. It was great fun because I got to eat all the cookies I could handle!

Dad worked his way up from cookie salesman to general manager of the company. With a seventh-grade education he managed one of the largest wholesale food companies anywhere. When Mom and Dad made the decision to buy the Cookson General Store and move to Lake Tenkiller, the CEO of L. D. Jones told Dad he could name his price if only he would stay on and run the company. Fortunately for all of us, Dad turned the lucrative offer down and we left Oklahoma City and moved to the lake.

Our heavenly Father also gives us lessons in His Word concerning hard work. In fact, He tells us to work six days and rest one. God loves hardworking Christians. He knows these are the ones who are willing to roll up their sleeves and do His work also. The harvest is plentiful but the workers are few. God depends on those willing to work!

PRAYER

Father, we may have been given dads who were loving and caring and great teachers, but ultimately the greatest teacher is Jesus.

LISTENING TO THE TEACHER

> Rejoice always, pray without ceasing, in everything give thanks; for this is the will of God . . . for you.
>
> -1 THESSALONIANS 5:16-18

If you hang around fishing tournaments, you soon learn there's a lot of talk going on. Some guys are just about to pop wanting to tell someone how many fish they caught and how. Others are talking about what they're doing, and some are actually just listening.

Learning to listen, knowing who to listen to, and being able to search out the real meaning in what they say can be invaluable tools to a tournament fisherman. Developing these learning skills can provide you with knowledge that is free for the taking. But you must be able to determine what folks are really saying.

Jesus taught in parables so the people could easily understand His meanings and lessons. Still, many did not perceive and refused to listen to His message. Jesus is talking to us today, if we'll only learn to listen and place that desire to understand first in our hearts and minds.

Reading God's Word on a daily basis is the simplest way to hear what God is saying. I promise you, if you read God's Word regularly, God will speak to you in everyday situations. He'll guide you to make decisions in your family, personal, and business relationships that will benefit everything you do. He'll give you the words to say when comforting a friend or leading another to Christ. He'll talk to you. All you have to do is listen.

The other way we can listen to God is with prayer. When we pray, all we

need to do is stop and listen to what God is telling us as we pray. Many times God has answered my prayers in the midst of a prayer. All I needed to do was listen for the answer.

PRAYER

Lord, we pray that You will instill in our hearts the desire to listen and obey the commandments You have given us to live by. From that will come great strength and peace.

OBEYING THE TEACHER

> You shall walk after the LORD your God and fear Him.
>
> -DEUTERONOMY 13:4

Charlie Ingram and I kid about being each others' fishing coach. I call him Coach and vice versa. In reality, we've have learned a lot from each other over the years. The coach "bit" started in 1986 at the final tournament of the year on Lake Chickamauga in Tennessee. I won the BASS-Angler-of-the-Year title that year but really should have won that final event and the $75,000 first-place money.

The tournament was a four-day event cutting down to the top fifty for the final day. I had the biggest catch the second and third days and was firmly in second place—only three ounces behind the

leader, Zell Rowland. I was locking through into Lake Nickajack and running forty miles down river to my "honey hole." Another good limit was almost a certainty—and another good limit meant victory!

The tournament director warned us about a boat race about ten miles down the lake. If we locked through, he cautioned, we probably wouldn't make it back through the locks in time for weigh-in. My coach, Charlie, told me I had to go! I had to take the chance. If I didn't make it back, so be it. He insisted I obey his guidance.

But the next morning I made the decision not to chance the locks. I caught two small bass that day and slipped to ninth place in the tour-nament. It was a great year with a first place, a second-place, a fourth-, and a fifth-place finish. But not obeying the teacher cost me a vic-tory that was there for the taking.

I'm constantly amazed how God's teachings are involved in every single thing that happens every day of my life. There isn't a prob-lem, a relationship, a feeling, not a thing that isn't covered in God's Holy Bible. There have been thou-sands of self-help books written telling us how to think, act, talk, and just about everything else. All of these teachings, in all of these books, can't come close to God's teachings. We're only asked to do two things: trust and obey. What a loving and caring Teacher!

PRAYER

Lord God, thank You for the successes we have in our lives and thank You for teaching us to obey the Teacher, Jesus Christ.

THE BASIC THOUGHT IN FISHING

By this gospel you are saved, if you hold firmly
to the word I preached to you.

-1 CORINTHIANS 15:2 NIV

If I were to ask you for the basic thought in fishing, your immediate answer would probably be "to catch fish." For a tournament angler, I guess that might always be true. For most others, though, fishing is so much more than just catching fish.

I recall a day a couple of years back, fishing on Lake Tenkiller with a young man from Tulsa: Stephen Maxwell. I had known Stephen since he was a small boy. He had come to the Tulsa Boat Show every year to visit me and tell me about fishing trips with his dad. Finally, after many years, we got to fish together. It seemed like every moment of that day was special. Stephen was having a dream come true, and I was having fun every minute of it. We didn't catch many fish, but what a great day! Yes, the basic thought in fishing can be a lot more than catching fish.

The basic thought in Christianity is the gospel of Jesus Christ. The gospel that allows us to live a relationship with God on an every-day-real-life basis. By trusting in Jesus and truly repenting of our sins, God instantly changes us into a new person. When we ask Jesus to save us and come in and take control of our lives, He does just that. He doesn't bargain or deal this salvation, He gives it to us bought and paid for. What is required is *faith*: faith to believe and faith to grow.

PRAYER

Father, place in us the faith not only to believe all the Word,
but to grow through that belief so that we might
experience fully all the things You are doing in our lives.

INFLUENTIAL ROLE MODELS

> Become an offering acceptable to God,
> sanctified by the Holy Spirit.
>
> -ROMANS 15:16 NIV

During the course of the year, I'll do close to one hundred personal appearances and fish several tournaments. I visit with literally thousands of fishermen both young and old. A recurring theme among so many of the young fishermen these days is their desire to have my job—to be just like Jimmy Houston. A lot of their parents feel just the same way. It's flattering, and I consider it a real honor.

This also has a positive effect on how I conduct myself. If someone wants to be just like you, it makes sense to try to be someone worth emulating. I think it's impossible not to be a role model. No matter how important or famous you are or how unimportant you think you are, someone is learning how to act from you. After all, famous people are not the most influential role models. This honor goes to moms and dads, grandmas and granddads, brothers, sisters, aunts, uncles, and so forth.

The deal is, we can all be good role models, or we can be bad ones. Someone is always watching and learning.

The greatest role model of all time is Jesus. We learn to become more Christlike when we study His life and discover our shortcomings. Next, we lay these shortcomings at the foot of the cross and ask God to mold us into the kind of person He wants us to be. I think it's important to continually pray

for God's help in all of this. He has the power to make us better and the promise to make us perfect one day.

PRAYER
Lord God, we pray that we will follow Your ways in all that we do.

DAILY PRACTICES

> Oh come, let us worship and bow down;
> let us kneel before the LORD our Maker.
>
> -PSALM 95:6

Professional tournament fishermen fish 200 to 250 days a year—that's a lot of practice. Many aspiring pros don't practice nearly that much. That's why so many are still aspiring.

Two years ago, Chris and I were practicing for an FLW tournament on Lake Okeechobee in Florida. We had allotted two days to practice before the actual tournament. I became so frustrated those two days because I literally couldn't hit the water. I hadn't touched a rod in a couple of months, and my presentation was horrible. I was only making good casts about 20 percent of the time. Most of the time my lure wasn't even close, and I must have been a really bad fishing partner—at least that's

what Chris kept saying all week! Worst of all, my lack of practice kept me out of the top ten.

Becoming the kind of Christian you want to be—and God wants you to be—takes practice also. And just like fishing, it's difficult to stay at the top of your game. The Devil makes it so easy for us to stumble, and getting us to miss church is one of his easiest weapons. Miss a few services and you find yourself slipping into the Devil's trap. Your attitudes toward others and toward God begin to change. You actually begin to lose some of the joy God has promised.

Obviously, daily practice includes prayer and reading the Bible. It's amazing how little time it takes to

read the Bible all the way through in a year—actually about five minutes each day. In that five minutes, God has something to say to you that will make your day and your practice of the Christian faith a whole lot better!

PRAYER

Lord, we know that communication with You through Your Word is the way You desire for us to live our lives. Help us to study Your Word every day.

PART FOUR

THE EQUIPMENT OF FISHING

The rod is the centerpiece of fishing. It's pretty hard to go fishing without one. The gospel is the centerpiece of Christianity. It's impossible to be a Christian without it. Like that first fishing rod, the gospel is really simple.

THE ROD

The fishing rod, I suppose, was developed by a great fisherman some time back by merely cutting a limb off a tree. This first rod was the only tool this guy actually needed to catch a fish. He didn't have a reel or line or Terminators or Excalibur lures. He had no chemically-sharpened hooks. He cut his rod from a tree, sharpened the end, and speared his catch. I bet it didn't take him too long to figure out how to carve a barb on the end of the hook to keep the fish from falling off. After all, if he didn't do well in that day's "tournament," he had to go without supper.

The most preferred rods now have come a long way. Most are graphite with the most popular bait-casting and spinning rods for bass at six to seven feet in length, or as short as five feet for ultralite fishing. Straight-handle rods are the most popular. We have developed a six-foot pistol-grip rod in the new Shimano Jimmy Houston Signature Series. This rod is primarily designed for spinnerbaits and for dead accurate casting. The pistol grip allows you to underhand cast more effectively, increasing your accuracy in tight situations.

I use mostly six-foot and six-and-a-half-foot rods in a medium heavy action. These rods allow for great accuracy plus delivery as I can make a nice quiet presentation of my lure to the fish. These lengths are also more effective in fighting and landing fish. I've seen a lot of fish lost next to the boat because the angler was using too long a rod.

Unlike fishing rods, the gospel hasn't changed in the nearly 2000 years since Jesus walked on earth. When we turn to Him, all our sins are forgiven; the really big bad ones, as well as those little ones that seem insignificant. The Bible tells us God remembers our sin no more. So, no matter how far you can cast with your favorite rod, God can throw all your sins even farther. And when you place your trust in Him, He promises He will do exactly that.

PRAYER

Father, the centerpiece of our lives is Jesus Christ—a gift from You that we never deserved. Thank you.

THE REEL

We proclaim [Christ], admonishing and teaching everyone with all wisdom.

-COLOSSIANS 1:28 NIV

Fishing reels today are a mixture of science, technology, physics, mathematics, and precious metals. They're a blend between a fine piece of jewelry and a work of art. The first casting reels were actually made by jewelers, and some of today's reels are certainly in the price range of a lot of artwork.

A fishing reel is one piece of equipment where you get what

you pay for. A good rule of thumb is to buy the best reel you can afford. This holds double true even if you're buying for your kids or your wife. Don't start them out with a cheap casting reel. Get them something good, and it will save a lot of frustration.

I fish with two weights in the out position, which leaves the other four snapped inward. This gives me a very fast reel on the out and allows me to cast as far as I want with very little effort or force. You never catch a fish as your lure is flying through the air on the cast. This is one place where the fastest reel on the out will give you several more casts during a tournament day. This little advantage will help you catch more fish.

We use a reel to present the lure to the fish. As believers, we also use our daily lives to present Christianity to the world. When you become a Christian, you become a role model whether you like it or not. The whole world is watching how you act and react, how you think, how you talk, and what kind of decisions you make.

God tells us not to be a stumbling block to the lost. Our actions can be that stumbling block. Our actions can also be the greatest witness for Christ that those around us have ever seen.

PRAYER

Father, because of the presence of Jesus Christ, I have the desire to present myself as a testimony to the lost and unbelieving, and I receive that strength through Jesus.

THE LINE

Your fishing line is a very important part of your fishing gear. It's the only thing between you and the fish, and a broken line means a lost fish.

I wind on new line every couple of months. That's a pretty good rule of thumb—new line every two to two-and-a-half months during the fishing season. I use backing and only take off about the top fifty yards. That means a 330-yard spool will fill about six reels. That's pretty cheap so get the best line you can buy. Also, fill your reels up all the way!

A frustrating thing about fishing line is there's not a line made that is best in all situations. All lines have both positives and negatives. Spinning reels require a soft, limp line in order to cast well and not tangle. But this soft line frays easily on rocks and brush. I use Trilene XL on spinning reels—and XL stands for extra limp. But most bass fishing is done around a lot of heavy cover, and in this heavy stuff you need a much harder, more abrasion-resistant line. This is where I use casting reels and Trilene XT—extra tough. This line doesn't work as well on spinning reels, but on casting equipment it handles great.

Line color is also important. I use low visibility green. The pros call it "Mean Green Trilene." I'm not sure if the fish can see it or not but it's the only color we can't photograph with our video cameras. Underwater, for our cameras, it's just not there!

As our fishing line connects us to our lure and ultimately to the fish, so the Bible connects us to God. Unlike line, however, the Bible is the perfect Word of God and cannot be improved upon. It's valuable for all situations and in all circumstances. The more we learn to rely on God's Word to lead us in everything we do, the more we realize just how perfect it is. It doesn't do us a lot of good, however, if it's lying on a shelf collecting dust.

As you immerse yourself in God's Word, you'll find its teachings and guidance coming more quickly into your heart and mind. That guidance will teach you why it's called the Living Bible.

PRAYER

Father, thank You for the Bible—our direct line to You.

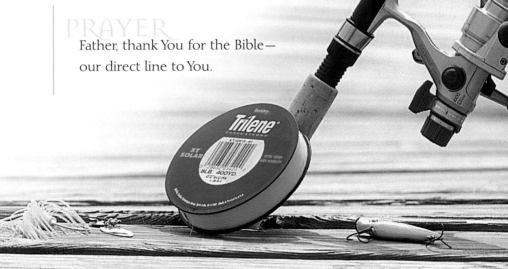

THE BOAT

The Spirit is given to each one for the profit of all.

-1 CORINTHIANS 12:7

Our first bass boat wasn't too fancy. In fact it wasn't really a bass boat at all. It was a fourteen-foot Lone Star aluminum V bottom with a twelve-horse Sea King motor. I didn't even own the boat; it belonged to my dad, but I could use it whenever I wanted. From my senior year in high school through college, I used it almost every day. This was back in the early sixties and there really wasn't such a thing as a bass boat.

We had it fixed up pretty neat though. We clamped on cushioned seats and installed a flat bottom inside the boat with boards. We had an old Silvertroll electric motor, which I clamped on the side of the boat toward the front. It was the only boat on the lake with a trolling motor on the front. This was years before we had twenty-four-volt trolling motors. You know though, we sure caught a lot of fish out of that old boat!

If you can learn to stop your boat where the fish are, you'll love this fishing game. Someone once said Roland Martin wasn't really that great, he just always had his boat parked where there were a bunch of bass.

Some churches are like a beautiful bass boat that's parked in the wrong spot. They're not doing much to reach out to the lost. My family and I attend a dynamic church where we see God at work on a daily basis. God has equipped His people with gifts that have the power to accomplish almost anything. What we need to do is put Jesus first in our lives and ask God what He wants us to do. He will lead us and our churches into some really exciting territory. Ask God today what more you can do in your church. He has a plan, and it's perfect!

PRAYER

Lord, thank You for giving us gifts that we can use to serve You.

THE FISH LOCATOR

Standard equipment on any bass boat is a fish locator and generally two or three at that—one on the console and one on the bow. My console unit now is a Humminbird NS25, which is a combination GPS (Global Positioning System) and liquid crystal chart locator. These units are really something. The GPS gives you your boat position, speed, time, and date. It allows you to mark spots, chart courses, and much more. It utilizes C-maps to give you a map of where you're fishing and helps you navigate via satellite configurations. The built-in chart locator is the best that's been developed and allows you to really know what's under your boat. Amazingly, these units are still simple to use.

Like most serious bass fishermen, I also have a flasher unit on my console. This is a big help in running and fishing grass. My locator up front is a Humminbird Panorama. I always have my front transducer mounted on my trolling motor. It's very important to know the depth and what is located under the front of the boat. Many times this is quite different from the back of the boat where the console transducers are mounted.

Make sure to have temp gauges, if available, in all of your units. You'll find that temperature changes are often the secret that unlocks a great area and allows you to catch a lot of fish. One of the most important things to learn is to watch your locator at all times as you fish and as you run. This is a habit you must get into in order to be successful. Learn to know always, out of the corner of your eye, what that locator is reading.

Faith in God is much like a fish locator. You are visualizing through your locator the structure and fish that you can't really see. You can't really see or touch the promises of God, but your faith allows you to see clearly what God is all about. We have faith that Heaven is real and Jesus has gone ahead of us to prepare a place for us in heaven. That same faith allows us to have confidence in God's control of our lives. But we must realize that God doesn't just come in and take control; we have to *surrender* to His will.

I find my most difficult and trying times to be when I'm trying to solve all my own problems and run my own life. I struggle with this because I know God wants to handle it all. When we humble ourselves and turn our lives over to God, He takes the burden. We can feel it in our hearts and be assured of His presence. Faith— the hope for things unseen—can actually be *seen* very clearly.

PRAYER

Oh, Father, we thank You and praise You for the wonderful gift of seeing Jesus in our lives and knowing the joy of peace because He is in control.

THE MOTOR

God is my strength and power, and He makes
my way perfect.

-2 SAMUEL 22:33

At the price of a small car or truck, our outboard motors today are true technological wonders. Most fishermen are still using electronic fuel-injected engines but the trend is definitely to the new direct fuel-injected motors. Environmentally friendly and unbelievably gas and oil efficient, these big power plants are high-tech wonders.

Our first actual bass boat was a fifteen-foot Terry Bass Boat with stick steering and a huge fifty-horsepower Mercury. We used that little boat and motor until I met Forrest and Nina Wood at the BASS Tournament in Eufaula, Alabama. Forrest talked me into buying a Ranger. It was the first Ranger boat in Oklahoma, and I

bought a 100 horsepower in-line six-cylinder Mercury to put on it. My dealer said we needed a power trim unit on that large engine, but that was an extra hundred dollars or so and we didn't have the money. I told him Chris and I would just lift the motor when we got in shallow water. But it took both of us to lift the engine and put it on its tilt bracket, and then we could barely do it. After three or four fishing trips, I took the rig back to my dealer and told him we needed that trim unit. We still didn't have the money, but I promised him that if he would put it on, we would gladly pay him when we could. He did, and we eventually paid it off.

In 1983, we started an organization called FOCAS, to worship God and take the gospel to tournaments.

FOCAS was started at a BASS event on Truman Lake as a Bible study group for the touring pros. Not only has it grown into a national ministry of fishermen, it has brought the gospel of Jesus Christ to many tournaments. We now average around one hundred attendees at each tournament. Many, many fishermen have been saved during these meetings.

Jesus used fishermen as his hand-chosen disciples and is still doing so today. When you see such superstars as Mark Davis, Jay Yelas, Guy Eaker, Shaw Grigsby, and others taking time out to worship God right in the middle of a national tournament, it's a great witness.

Whatever you're involved in, make sure God is a visible part of that activity.

PRAYER

Thank You, Father, for the privilege of being hand-chosen disciples and for the eternal life that goes with it.

PART FIVE

Casting

G od wants us to be happy and successful. He has set out the guidelines He knows will help us. The devil, on the other hand, possesses lures that are designed to make our life miserable. These lures may seem like the best or easiest to use at the time, but they are built for destruction and unhappiness.

WHAT TO CAST

The wisdom that is from above is first pure,
then peaceable, gentle, willing to yield, full of mercy.

-JAMES 3:17

One of the most important decisions you'll make on any fishing day is what lure to cast. I decide what to cast based on four criteria: the type of water, what that water is doing, the time of the year, and the weather.

A common mistake in lure selection is wanting to make the fish bite what you want them to as opposed to what *they* want. Change lures if your favorite doesn't work. Don't get into the habit of changing lures too often, however, as this is probably the second biggest mistake in lure selection. Choose your lures wisely and develop the confidence to stick with your decisions.

I generally have six or seven rods with four or five different types of baits tied on. I'll usually have three or four titanium spinnerbaits with size and blade configuration determining the difference. I'll have a worm or jig, a crankbait or two, and, depending on the situations, one or more topwater baits. This is a fairly basic setup that will serve you well in most situations. Granted, I may throw only one lure all day long but this variety will keep me from having to get into my tackle box very often.

What we cast upon the waters of life will have a determining factor on everything we do. We can choose godly lures like compassion, honesty, faithfulness, and so forth, or we can choose the Devil's lures such as jealousy, dishonesty, envy—this list goes on and on. With ample usage of God's lures, we can improve our relationships with our family, friends, and everyone we come in contact with. We can also develop a level of integrity in our business dealings that will lead to success.

Jesus saved us to set us apart from the world. He gave us gifts of the Holy Spirit to live a spirit-filled life. He doesn't want us to comform to the world but to be different from the world. He also gave us the power to resist the temptations of those "pretty lures" in the devil's tackle box.

PRAYER

Lord God, each day presents us with temptations, but You have given us a desire to do what is righteous and godly. We praise You.

CASTING FOR ACCURACY

Let your conduct be worthy of the gospel of Christ.

-PHILIPPIANS 1:27

Casting accuracy is one of the skills that separates pros from average fishermen. It's a highly developed skill to be able to throw a quarter-ounce bait thirty to forty feet and make it land precisely where you want it to.

In 1962, the World Series of Sports Fishing was held at my home, Lake Tenkiller. This was before BASS was formed. The best fishermen in the country were there to compete. They practiced two or three weeks, and I had the chance to fish with most of them. I fished with Jim Rogers, Glen Andrews, Joe Krieger, Roy Martin, and the legendary Virgil Ward.

What an opportunity for a skinny sixteen-year-old kid who loved to fish—to spend time in the boat with these guys. I learned a lot. But the thing I noticed most was their ability to place the lure exactly where they wanted. I made it my goal to learn how to do that.

Very early in my tournament career, I learned firsthand how important that is. I was fishing in the World Series of Sport Fishing five years later on Lake Texoma. My partner, a much more experienced fisherman, was running the trolling motor with "the kid" in the back. We were throwing topwaters, Heddon Chuggers. Close to weigh-in time, as we fished down the bank, we came to a small niche in the brush line that was narrow and set back a couple of feet. My partner had the first shot, but he missed the spot, so I fired my chugger back into the hole. Boom! A three-pounder nailed it. My partner had the first chance, but I caught the fish.

Accuracy is also important as we live our lives following God's laws. As Christians we are being watched closely by the world. We must work hard to live as Jesus would have us live. Yes, we do fail sometimes, but with God's help and guidance we have the opportunity to be the kind of example the world needs.

PRAYER

Father, we are the only Bible some folks will ever read. Help us to lead a godly life that will bring praise and glory to You.

HOW MANY CASTS ARE ENOUGH?

So let us not grow weary in doing what is right, for we will reap at harvest time, if we do not give up.

-GALATIANS 6:9 NRSV

Multiple casts are part of learning to become a good bass fisherman. When we talk about multiple casts, we're talking about making more than one cast to the same spot; perhaps a lot more casts. I've actually seen many instances where bass will strike only after repeated casts to the same spot. Usually this will be the second or third cast. Even when bass are aggressive, some still won't bite on the first throw. Generally, these are the bigger bass, the ones you'd really like to catch.

During the BASSMASTERS Classic in Louisville, I tossed a spinnerbait back in a little nook among some tie-up pilings. A two-and-a-half pounder swirled on the bait but missed. I told my press observer to get ready, I was going to catch that fish. Quickly, I changed rods and chunked a plastic worm in the hole. No strike! Again and again, no strike. After twenty or thirty throws my observer commented, "That bass is history!"

I went back to the spinnerbait, another twenty to thirty casts, and then back to the worm. The observer put his camera down and went back to reading. I don't know how long it took or how many casts—definitely over one hundred—but, finally, that old bass nailed that spinnerbait like he'd never seen one before.

When we're sharing God's Word, we certainly don't want to give up if our first attempt falls on deaf ears or hardened hearts. Think about it. How many people respond positively to the gospel their first opportunity? Not very many. They hear about it through conversation, in a sermon, or in a testimony or song. Perhaps someone is praying for them. All are different casts of Jesus' salvation message into hearts that need Him.

Why should we give up after our first attempt? God didn't give up on us until we responded to Him. Our task is to "chunk and wind" every chance we get. Keep on praying, keep on loving and offering the gospel. That one last cast may be just the one to land a "big 'un."

PRAYER

Lord, don't let me grow tired of telling the story of salvation.

PART SIX

LURE SELECTION

Life is full of lures that can lead us in all directions. Some are the best. These are lures designed by God. Others are way down the list and can be downright terrible. There are lures designed by the devil and may look enjoyable at the moment but will lead to a path of destruction.

For the grace of God that brings salvation has appeared to all men, teaching us that, denying ungodliness and worldly lusts, we should live . . . righteously.

-TITUS 2:11-12

I guess every fisherman is looking for that magic lure, the one that will catch the biggest fish and the most fish. That's why some gimmick lures have been so successful for short periods of time. They make promises that are too good to be true, but are just what fishermen have always hoped for.

In fishing, there is no magic lure. No matter how many lures you own, you've got to decide which one to use. If you only own ten lures, the

decision is relatively simple: one is the best for the situation right now, one is the worst, and the other eight are somewhere in between. Study the type of water you're fishing and determine the best lures for that type. Next, check out what the water is doing. Is it rising? Falling? Getting warmer or cooler? Clearing up or getting murky? Remember, water is always doing something. Based on the water conditions, you should be able to eliminate a lot of lures. With what's left, consider what baits work best at that particular time of the year. This will eliminate even more. Finally, check out the weather to determine your best lure choice.

Speaking of making choices, every choice we make in life has the possibility of changing our lives forever. This is sometimes difficult to realize at the time, but a close walk with God will always help us in these decisions. When we stray away from a day-by-day relationship with Jesus, the devil will pull one of his lures out of the tackle box. Sometimes it's such a subtle offering, we don't even recognize where it's coming from. And by the time we do, our lives may be changed forever. So stay in close contact with God—because with His Word, life's decisions will become much simpler.

PRAYER
Father, Your Spirit drew us to the cross. We thank You for the grace we have so abundantly received in our newness of life.

SPECIAL LURES, SPECIAL CONDITIONS

Send out Your light and Your truth! Let them lead me.

-PSALM 43:3

Fish very much and you'll encounter just about every condition possible with the elements, water, and fishing pressure. So far, no one has come up with a lure that is best under all conditions. That's why our tackle boxes are full of lures!

One of the toughest factors of all is the dreaded cold front. Most cold fronts happen pretty much the same way and do the same things to the bass. As a front pushes in, the barometer drops rapidly, accompanied by rain and high wind. As the front passes, the clouds roll away and the wind subsides, leaving a clear, "bluebird" day. Bass usually feed heavy during the approaching front but are difficult to catch once the front passes.

My lure choice for this situation is one I can work slowly and meticulously in the heaviest possible cover. That lure is a jig with pork or plastic attached. Also, depending on available cover, a slow-rolled spinnerbait or a slow moving crankbait will work well.

Another thing to remember is that, generally, bass will not leave a location. They merely move into the thickest part of the cover, and their strike zone becomes smaller. This, of course, means a slow presentation with dead accurate multiple casts.

Another tricky condition is extremely clear water. Bass tend to be more finicky and choosy about what they eat. If your choice is a spinnerbait, go with a smaller bait: willow leaf blades for a quiet approach and skirt colors that are basically clear or translucent. A good choice in topwater would be a clear Pop-R or Crazy Shad. These baits basically disappear to the fish except for the flash of the hooks and props. A curly-tail Road Runner also works well.

We also encounter tough conditions in our lives: serious illness, death, disability. Only God's love and strength and our hope in eternal life can sustain us at these times. Other special conditions happen more casually with family, friends, co-workers, and even strangers. It may be as simple as a disagreement or harsh words at the breakfast table or another driver cutting you off on your way to work. Our reaction in every situation can, and should, be led by God's Holy Spirit. We need to let Him take over, and the fruit of the Spirit will make us better people.

PRAYER

Father, we pray that You will continue to lead us and teach us how to live our lives in accordance with Your Word.

DOES COLOR MAKE A DIFFERENCE?

> The message of the cross is foolishness to those who are perishing, but to us who are being saved it is the power of God.
>
> -1 CORINTHIANS 1:18

Color is special to fishermen. As a matter of fact, the very next question after "what did you catch them on" is generally "what color?" And, indeed, color is important to fish.

Dr. Loren Hill has done extensive studies at the University of Oklahoma on how fish perceive color. These studies determined that fish can distinguish and choose colors under all light and water conditions. The fish will choose the color they can see best. From these studies, Dr. Hill developed the Color-C-Lector to tell which color to use at any given time.

Does it work? Yes! I can cite many examples. Such as the time Chris and I were fishing on Lake Dardanelle in Arkansas. It was spring and the lake was extremely muddy. We tried all the usual muddy-water colors such as chartreuse, fluorescent red, and fluorescent orange. We had fished all morning without a single strike. About noon, Chris pulled out the Color-C-Lector and dropped the probe into the water. "Purple" she said. "This thing shows purple! No way! That's about the last color that would work today." But she tied on a purple spinnerbait and made eight or ten casts. Would you believe a five-pounder rolled out from under a log and sucked in that purple spinnerbait? It doesn't take me long to recognize a horseshoe! I tied on a purple spinnerbait, and we proceeded to catch about twenty bass that weighed over eighty pounds total. Color does make a difference!

What makes a difference in a Christian's life? Jesus makes a difference. And the difference He makes has a strong correlation to how close we walk with Him. Jesus promised that when we place our trust in Him, He saves us and places His Spirit inside us. We don't have to hope to receive God's Spirit, it's a guarantee!

PRAYER

Father, thank You for the indwelling Holy Spirit and the impact He has in our daily lives. We know this is by Your grace.

DEEP-RUNNING LURES

> Narrow is the gate and difficult is the way which
> leads to life, and few there are who find it.
>
> -MATTHEW 7:14

As long as a lure doesn't float, any lure can become a deep-running lure. Some guys even put floating lures on a Carolina rig, and they become deep-diving lures. A spinnerbait can certainly become deep-diving if cranked slowly and allowed to sink; so can a jig or worm. But, ultimately, when I think deep-diving lures, I think crankbaits.

There are lots of ways to be successful with a deep-diving crankbait. One of the easiest is jumping points: going from point to point and casting into shallow water and retrieving back into deeper water. Early in the year, before the spawn, this is about all that you need to know about bass fishing.

One of my favorite techniques, though, I used during the 1997 BASS Top 100 Tournament on Old Hickory Lake near Nashville. This technique involves finding the first primary drop in an area then following that drop with a depth finder. In some instances, drops are out on the main lake. These particular drops were in a major creek at nine feet. We were casting into deeper water and shallower water and bringing that bait both up and down the drop. We were using Bomber's Fat Free Shad and a Poe's 400 deep-diving crankbait.

The secret was to keep the boat in nine feet of water as we moved up and down the drop. Sometimes we were thirty yards from the bank and sometimes we were three hundred yards. Some casts would be into fifteen feet of water and some were in five. The key was to come up to nine feet or down to nine feet. As we moved along these nine-foot drops, we occasionally found a brush pile and frequently found bass in the brush piles—usually good ones.

God also wants His followers to keep on a straight and narrow pathway. The more we walk His way, the better He likes it. When we deviate from this we only cause problems in our lives.

If you're having difficulties, come back to God's way—that's where the solutions always are.

PRAYER

Lord, keep us on the path—the straight and narrow path that takes us to eternal life.

SHALLOW-RUNNING LURES

Be diligent to present yourself approved to God,
a worker who does not need to be ashamed.

-2 TIMOTHY 2:15

Without a doubt, most bass are caught in shallow water, less than ten feet deep—more often than not in five feet or less. That's why most bass lures are designed to be fished shallow. Many lures made to be fished deep can be effective in skinny water but spinnerbaits, jigs, and worms come quickly to mind as shallow bait, even though they can also be fished deep.

Shallow-running crankbaits fill the bill as true shallow baits. And speaking of the bill, some of the most effective shallow crankbaits have a square bill instead of a rounded one. This allows the bait to bump off of stumps, logs, and other shallow-water brush without getting hung up too much. This "bumping" into something is the best way to fish these baits. When you hear folks talking about a deflection strike, this is it. It causes an erratic action to the bait and quite often triggers a strike.

When I feel a crankbait bump into something, I like to pause the bait, simply stop reeling for a count of one or two, then continue. The sound of the bait hitting some obstruction and the deflected action gets the bass's attention. The pause gives the bass a chance to catch up to the bait. Another little trick with these lures is to cut off the front portion of the front treble hook. This actually makes it a double hook. Since you cut the front part off, it lets the bait slide over brush and doesn't get hung up as often.

You don't need to use shallow crankbaits in hard cover areas only. They are also excellent grass baits.

When you find you can crank these baits over the top of submerged grass, by all means, do so! The best is when you can just tip the top of the grass with the bait. Sometimes, this will catch bass when they won't touch a spinner-bait or worm.

A shallow Christian is what the world calls a *hypocrite*—a stumbling block to those who are lost. It's professing to be a Christian and living like the devil. It's impossible to live perfect lives. We all mess up on a daily basis, and I probably do more than most folks. But it's important to remember that someone is always watching to see how we react to any situation.

PRAYER

Father, You know all that is in our hearts, and You know our love for You. We ask You to strengthen that love and cleanse our hearts of all sinful thoughts and desires.

CONFIDENCE

I can do all things through Christ who strengthens me.
-PHILIPPIANS 4:13

It's been said many times that confidence is the number one lure in the tackle box. That statement has a lot of truth in it. It's difficult to have much success with a bait in which you have no confidence. But it's easy to stick with a bait you really believe in. *Confidence* is just another word for faith. But how do we develop faith in what we're doing or what lure we're using?

Mostly, we're fishing for bass we can't see, so we're relying totally on faith. This faith or confidence is developed through past experiences and knowledge. When a method or lure works, confidence is built for

future trips. As you learn more about what you're doing, your confidence will increase.

Some frequently asked questions are, How do you know when to change baits? How do you know when to change colors? How do you know when to change places? It seems obvious to me that there is no pat answer. In fact, one question really works against the other. If we have a great deal of confidence in the lure we're fishing and believe it's our number one choice for that particular situation, we need to change places pretty quick if we aren't getting any bites. If, however, we believe we're in the right place and there are plenty of fish in that spot, we had better be changing lures and/or tactics if we're not having much success.

God wants us to be confident, and we should be confident. We should be able to build faith that can move a mountain. Yet, our confidence is sometimes shaken by our failures or the failures of those we love or admire. But, God doesn't change. He's still there walking beside us, carrying us if need be. He has the solution for our failures. He has answers to our problems, our prayers, and our shortcomings. I'm confident that my God can do anything and will do whatever is best in every situation in my life, both now and forever.

PRAYER

Thank You Mighty God for Your promises. And thank You even more for keeping them—as You always have and always will.

PART SEVEN

FINDING FISH

The problem is, most of the time you can't see the fish, and you're fishing where you think (or hope) they are. The trick is to find out what is important to the bass and make that important to you. Folks say this is learning to think like a bass, but I'm not sure bass can think. It might be more like learning to think like a bass *lives*.

GET A MAP

Without maps, professional tournament fishing would be a difficult game to play. The tournament game has become such that an angler who lacks good map-reading skills is working with a handicap. The maps that give you the most information are topographical maps. These show bottom contours as well as the normal creeks, rivers, bays, etc., that other maps show.

A lot of maps nowadays were made especially for fishing. They usually cost a bit more but offer much additional helpful information: bottom contour, brush piles, boat ramps, gas docks, camping areas, and even hot spots for certain species of fish. Some even have fishing tips for different times of the year and types of lures and colors. Most of these maps are waterproof and will last a long time.

Topographical or contour maps are sometimes difficult to learn to read. A little tip is to color between the lines with a colored marker. For instance color zero to ten feet red; ten to twenty feet green; and so forth. Do this with the entire lake and the map will literally come alive; it will be much easier to read. Underwater points, humps, and bends in creeks will stand out.

The latest in maps are GPS (Global Positioning Systems) that utilize C-Map cartridges. These don't show bottom contour but are great for navigating while the boat is moving. It's wonderful to be able to follow a lake map at sixty-five miles per hour.

God's map for us is the Bible. It will always show us where we need to go. Like a map, its purpose is to keep us from being lost. God has always been showing man the way by miraculous means. The Bible today is no less miraculous than the pillar of fire that led Moses or the star that led the shepherds and Wise Men to Jesus.

A good map can't catch the fish, but it can show you where they live. The Bible can't save you, but it can lead you to the One who can—Jesus.

PRAYER

Dear God, we marvel at the teachings of Jesus and how His Word guides us in our Christian walk each day.

We know that all things work together for
the good to those who love God, to those who
are called according to His purpose.

-ROMANS 8:28

I 've heard it said a million times that anyone can catch fish—the trick is to find them. There must be a lot of truth to that because most of the folks who don't catch them very often comment, "I can catch fish as good as anybody, I just can't find them."

In the spring, the most important thing to the bass is spawning. In the early part of this process, they move to points near bends in the creek or river channels. They then migrate down the sides of pockets or coves to good spawning areas. These areas generally have gentle

sloping banks with sandy or gravel bottoms, and they usually face south. These are the places to look for bass in the spring.

In the summer or fall, the most important thing is food. Finding the bass might be as simple as finding the bait fish or a bank with a lot of crawdad holes in it. In a clear lake, a bass might want to seek out some dingy water in order to catch his dinner more easily. Find that dingy water, and you'll find him. Think how the bass lives and what is important to him and make that important to you. More often than not, you'll find fish.

Let's think about what is important to the believer's life. Jesus said the most important thing is *love*. If that is the most important thing to Jesus, it should be the most important thing to us. The Bible says that love covers a multitude of sins, and we've all committed a multitude. Christians are often called right-wing extremists. If you're going to be an extreme on something, be extreme on love. Remember, those sins that love covers are not just your own. They are also the sins others have committed against you. Let the love of Jesus in you cover the sins of someone today.

PRAYER

Lord, each day is not always what we want it to be. But, we know that it is all for a purpose that fulfills Your perfect plan.

WHERE TO LOOK

God did not send His Son into the world
to condemn the world, but that the world
through Him might be saved.

-JOHN 3:17

One of the neatest things in bass fishing is to catch a bass exactly where you thought he would be. It's so cool to look at a piece of structure and picture in your mind exactly where that fish is positioned, place your lure exactly in that spot, and BAM! That's what bass fishing is all about. Most of the better fishermen seldom catch a bass in a place that surprised them.

I love to fish rivers and creeks. These are places where you have a great opportunity to find exactly where the fish are located. A large creek becomes a lake itself for most bass. They live

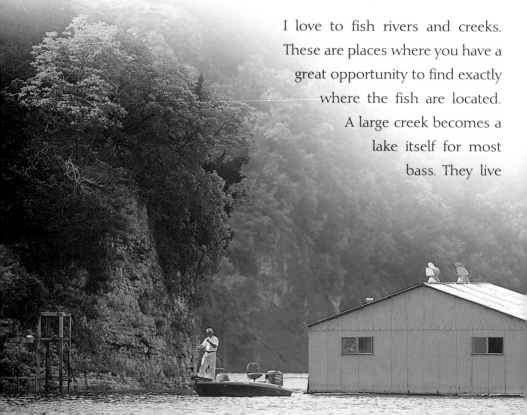

their entire life there without ever leaving. If there's a good population of fish in that creek, you can pretty much have success there year round.

If the creek or river has a current flow, and most do, you know that bass always face upstream. This will let you know which way a bass is facing on any particular piece of cover, so you can cast your lure to the front of the bass where his mouth is. You'll get more bites bringing the lure to the front of the bass.

You also need to be aware of junction areas, where bass tend to lie and wait for something to eat. Some common junction areas are corners of boat docks, two logs crossing each other, a limb coming off a log, or a piece of brush. In other words, any spot where two pieces of structure form a junction.

As neat as it is to catch a bass right where you thought you should, it's also neat to watch God solve a problem for you, to see the miraculous turn of events He uses to make it happen. Nothing is too big or too complicated for God. I've seen God put together a whole string of events that seemed almost impossible, just to make sure someone got saved. That's the kind of God I serve.

PRAYER

Father, we stand in awe of the greatness of Your love for us. We thank You for Your presence in our lives.

PATTERNS THAT PRODUCE FISH

Love your enemies, bless those who curse you, do good to those who hate you, and pray for those who spitefully use you.

-MATTHEW 5:44

The key to catching fish and doing well in tournament competition is figuring out a pattern that will produce fish. A pattern could be as simple as fishing the shady side of all lay-down logs. Or catching bass only under cloud cover with a south wind, or throwing a certain color spinner-bait on the down current side of a live buck bush.

Generally, the simpler patterns are figured out by a lot of fishermen, but as a pattern becomes more complicated, fewer and fewer folks figure it out. Mark Menedez, from

Kentucky, won the 1997 BASS Top One Hundred tournament on Pickwick Lake near Florence, Alabama. He shared his pattern with me and helped me place high in the money.

He was fishing a blue/chrome Bomber Long A. He had it weighted perfectly so it would suspend but float up ever so slightly. He was fishing it slowly with an eight-pound line. He also told me the types of points to fish. All I needed to know was exactly where he was fishing so I wouldn't accidentally fish his waters. Sure, this was a complicated pattern, but Mark had it figured out better than anybody. Over the next two days, I caught big strings and zoomed up in the standings. But Mark won the tournament.

There's also a pattern to successful witnessing for Christ.

The key to that pattern is consistency: in the way we act, talk, think, and treat others. When we act loving and kind in one situation and angry and mean in another, it hampers our witness. When we treat one person like royalty and another like trash, our witness is inconsistent with the teachings of Jesus. You have been given the task of modeling the role of a disciple of Jesus. Don't change the pattern—be consistent.

PRAYER

Lord, let me live out what I say I believe every day. Let me be consistent in my pattern of living to point others to You.

KEEP A DIARY

> Be strong and of good courage; do not be afraid,
> nor be dismayed, for the LORD your God
> is with you wherever you go.
>
> -JOSHUA 1:9

Successful fishing is no more than repeating successful techniques. For example, if you have success fishing a Zara Spook on points after the spawn, you can probably duplicate that year after year and catch fish. It's like throwing a strike in bowling or hitting that perfect drive down the middle of the fairway. The difference is, you are looking to duplicate a set of conditions.

The easiest way to do this is to keep a record of your fishing trips to remind you of what worked and what didn't. Record things like where you fished (type of water), the date, weather, and what the water was doing. Jot down how you caught your fish, the time of day, depth, and the lure you used. You might also want to note what you tried that *didn't* work. You might also want to take a few pictures to keep in your fishing dairy. After you keep a diary for a few years, you'll be amazed at how simple it is to figure out the fish on your next trip.

Here's another tip: You can add value to your diary by recording what worked best for other folks. Multiply your information, and you'll be a better fisherman.

We also need to borrow on the successes and failures of others as we go through life. There are many examples in the Bible. One of my favorite characters is Joshua.

Joshua's success is directly related to the fact that he took God at His word, no matter what the circumstances. In addition, Joshua was a man's man. He had the courage and the leadership to include his family in serving the Lord.

As a husband and father, we lead the direction of our family. We can lead them to serve the Lord, as Joshua did, or we can lead them to serve the world. Becoming the godly man our family deserves should be one of our primary goals.

PRAYER

Thank You, Father, that as we learn Your ways and apply them to our lives, we grow stronger in our Christian life.

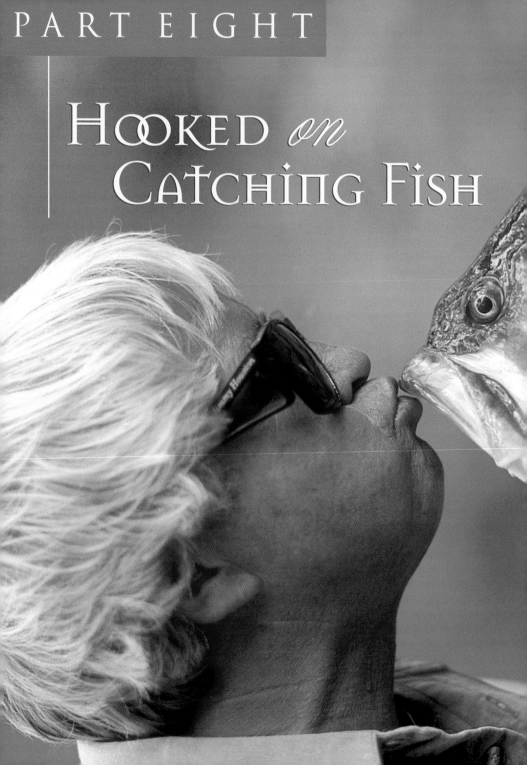

PART EIGHT

HOOKED *on*
CATCHING FISH

For those millions of fishermen who don't tournament fish, the rewards can be just as satisfying and the failures just as frustrating. Fishing is a challenge, and I guess the reward at any level is the accomplishment of a job well done.

THE REWARDS OF CATCHING FISH

His master replied, "Well done, good and faithful servant!"
-MATTHEW 25:23 NIV

To a bass fisherman the reward of catching fish is about pounds and ounces. Lots of pounds and ounces lead to winning—not catching fish leads to frustration.

Roland Martin and I were fishing for peacock bass in Venezuela a few years back, on Guri Lake, a huge lake of about three million acres. We were fishing in areas we had never seen before in our life, and we were having a tough time figuring out where the fish were. We tried the customary main lake areas the guides were suggesting but couldn't get a bite. I told Roland the fish were probably in a pre-spawn period. He agreed, and we set out to find water that might fit into that scenario.

We located a huge creek and looked for bays and small coves with distinct points as we motored up the creek. Sure enough, the first such place produced two nice peacock bass. The next tiny cove had three bass on one point and two on the other. The rest of the day, we caught bass every time we stopped the boat. Roland was also rewarded with catching his largest peacock bass ever: over fifteen pounds. As a bonus, we caught a small three-and-a-half-foot cayman on a Zara Spook.

In one of the parables Jesus told, the master leaves talents to his servants for safekeeping and growth. One servant doubles the five talents and produces five more. "Well done, good and faithful servant" is the master's reply. What a great goal it should be for us to have Jesus look us in the eye one day and say, "Well done, good and faithful servant."

As we encounter the stress and strain thrown at us by daily living, we need to keep this goal in mind. After all, Jesus has given us talents that are much more valuable than talents of gold. He has given us a physical and spiritual talent of love, joy, forgiveness, and so many more. Just like the talents of gold, we must not hide the talents given to us, but multiply them. We do this by sharing them with everyone we meet.

PRAYER

Father, may we live our lives in such a way that one day we will hear You say, "Well done."

FEELING THE BITE

I will instruct you and teach you
in the way you should go.

-PSALM 32:8

Every seminar on fishing generates questions about how the bite feels, especially on a plastic worm or jig. It's really quite easy to learn what a bite feels like: it feels different than the feeling of *not* having a fish on. After fishing any bait for just a few minutes, you'll learn what the bait feels like when a fish is not biting it. When that feeling changes, it's most likely a bite. It may be a jolt, a slight tick, a gentle tug, or simply dead weight—as if you had picked up a ball of grass or a sponge. If it feels different—set the hook!

Sometimes messages from God can be difficult to detect. Sometimes His message is a jolt, just like that bass about to get your rod. But mostly, God's messages are gentle tugs. Like leading us to the right verse in the Bible to help us through a problem period or make the correct decision. Or bringing the right person along to help us know His will, or leading us through whatever situation we're in at the moment. Whatever "bite" God uses, the closer we are to Him, the easier it will be to detect. If God isn't talking to you, it could be that a little more time in daily prayer and Bible reading will draw you closer to Him.

PRAYER

Father, we know that Your Word is the revelation of the teachings of Your Son, Jesus Christ. We pray that You will give us discernment of the Word and teach us how to live that Word daily.

SETTING THE HOOK

> Let us not love in word or tongue,
> but in deed and in truth.
>
> -1 JOHN 3:18

Hooksetting is one of the most important aspects of catching fish, and yet many fishermen do it improperly every time. Proper hooksets must be learned for the various techniques and lures.

In bass fishing, a Carolina rig hookset and a crankbait hookset can be pretty much the same. The best technique is to set the rod in a sideways motion. This pulls through the slip sinker on a Carolina rig and allows the most amount of force to reach the hook. It also works well on a crankbait as you have treble hooks, and you want to imbed as many points of each treble as you can in the bass.

For Texas rigged worms and jigs, the most important thing you're looking for is rod speed. To get a lot of force to the hookset, you must generate a lot of rod speed. The best way to do this is to keep your hands and reel in close to your body, square your shoulders to the fish, and set the hook in an upwards motion—remember to generate as much rod speed as you can.

The most frequently overlooked part of hooksetting is turning the reel handle at the finish of the hookset. Those two or three turns of the handle are the follow-through in hooksetting. Just as follow-through is vital in hitting a baseball or golfball, it is very important to a really great hookset. Hopefully, there's a really big bass waiting out there, and you can only turn the handle one time.

That one turn may make the difference between catching or losing the bass of a lifetime.

When we're able to lead someone to Christ, our job is not done—it's just started. We've got to follow-through to do our part in guiding this young Christian to maturity. It means making sure you invite him or her to church and Sunday school and other functions. Buying them a Bible or book from time to time to help them learn. Encouraging them in their day-to-day living.

PRAYER

Father, please teach us how to continue to feed the new lambs as they have received Your Son as their Lord and Savior.

TIMING IN HOOKSETTING

As for God, His way is perfect;
the word of the LORD is proven.

-PSALM 18:30

Fishing seminar speakers like to joke about when to set the hook—"when you get a bite" is the standard quip. That's true, but it's not quite that simple. Topwater fishing, for example, would get very frustrating if we jerked every time we saw a bass blow up on the bait. We have to wait until we feel the fish before we set the hook. That can be pretty hard to do, but until we learn to do it, we'll probably miss more bass than we catch.

Timing is especially critical with a floating worm or sluggo type bait. These are soft, plastic, single-hook lures. You don't lose many bass once you get them on, but it can sure be hard to hook a bass with one. The universal mistake is not waiting long enough to set the hook once the bass takes it. My advice is to count to three after you feel or see the bass take the bait. You've got to do this like a southern boy and not like a fast-talking auctioneer. I'm talking ooonnneee, tttwwwooo, ttthhhreee . . . SET THE HOOK! Now the fish is hooked up and you'll probably put him in the boat.

Timing is also important in our relationship with God. I'm so guilty of wanting God to accomplish things in my life on my timetable and not His. Shortly after we started the television show over twenty years ago, ESPN became a small startup network devoted totally to sports. What a great idea! I knew it would work and wanted badly to have our fishing show on ESPN. They wanted it exclusively, which meant we would have to pull off of over seventy independent stations. We had to wait a while but, sure enough, I was right about ESPN. It grew, and when we finally got together a few years later, the timing was perfect for ESPN and for Jimmy Houston Outdoors.

Once again, God's timing was perfect. The Bible is full of instructions on waiting for God's plan and God's time. The great part is that He knows the plan, whether it's next week or years from now. And He's promised it will be for our good.

PRAYER

Father, we seek Your will in everything we do— in all our challenges and accomplishments. We want to live according to Your timetable.

CATCH AND RELEASE

> Do not let any unwholesome talk come out of your
> mouths, but only what is helpful for building others up.
>
> -EPHESIANS 4:29 NIV

Fishing pressure today is the greatest it's ever been. We have more fishermen fishing for every species in all parts of the country. With that said, fishing today is still the best ever and seemingly getting better. The reason is twofold: smaller limits with mandatory lengths, and voluntary catch and release programs.

I fish with a friend, Gary Van Pelt, who is the best catfisherman I've ever seen. He fishes for giant catfish, and he never keeps one. Last June we caught two over seventy pounds one day and another over eighty pounds. The first one we caught, I thought weighed over one hundred pounds. Gary said, "No, that fish weighs about seventy-eight pounds."

I asked, "How do you know?"

He answered, "I caught that fish last August and weighed it. It weighed seventy-three pounds and has probably gained five or six pounds since then."

You might want to try some catch and release with other species in addition to bass. It will improve the fishing where you fish in both size and quantity. By the way, that big catfish was probably over forty years old. What a shame to kill him!

One of the things believers are sometimes guilty of is leading someone to Christ but not releasing that person's past. God forgives every sin no matter what it was, and we need to forget it also. One of the most difficult facts for new Christians to believe is that God can actually cast those sins away and remember them no more. Well, He can, and we need to remind and encourage any new Christian of this every chance we get.

PRAYER

Father, help us to remind others of the love of Jesus Christ and the forgiveness that You freely give for all our sins.

SEEKING THE RIGHT PLACE

Take up the whole armor of God, that you may be able
to withstand in the evil day.

-EPHESIANS 5:13

We could write volumes about seeking the right place in fishing. This can range all the way from a specific part of the lake, down to an exact cast. It's those few inches that generally make the difference in catching a fish. In order to become a good bass fisherman we need to learn where those right places are. Then it's a matter of slowing down, concentrating, and making sure we are as close to perfect as possible in those potential strike zones. This can be fairly easy in shallow water, but it's a lot more difficult when the places are deep or on structure we can't see. It's just as important to be exact at ten or fifteen feet as it is at two.

Boat positioning is critical. Distance to the target is important, and of course being able to duplicate the same exact cast and angle every time is the secret to catching several fish in one spot. I recommend using marker buoys and laying out something on top of the water to give you reference points. With two or three marker buoys, you can pinpoint where you want to throw and where your boat is positioned.

If we're going to lead the kind of Christian life God wants us to live, we must learn how to be in the right place to avoid sin. The devil is the master deceiver and tempter. If he can get us in the right place, he can sometimes hook us into sin

easier than we can hook a bass. It's easy to attend parties or other social functions where things go on that can compromise Christian beliefs. When we walk in, the devil goes to work and tries to tempt us. I find the best way to avoid this is to lead a life where everyone around knows you belong to Christ.

PRAYER

Father, we know that our witness is important to those who have turned their backs on Jesus. Help us to be a godly witness.

TWO-WAY CONVERSATIONS

Therefore I tell you, whatever you ask for in prayer, believe that you have received it, and it will be yours.

-MARK 11:24 NIV

We listen to bass by noticing the basic reaction or non-reaction to what is happening around them. They may be "talking" pretty loudly when they viciously strike our lures yet don't get hooked. They may be hitting the bait with their mouths closed, or they may not be hitting it at all but only trying to scare it away. At any rate, they're telling us we need to change something in order to have them take the bait.

On a spinnerbait, one solution is to add a trailer to the lure, generally a fairly large trailer. If the water is clear, we may want to speed up our retrieve. If it's murky, we may want to slow it down. If it's a topwater, changing the cadence on the retrieve usually helps. The fish may only be "whispering" to us, and if we're not really tuned in and listening carefully we probably won't hear it. We might catch a glimpse of a bass following our bait. We may feel the vibration change on a crankbait as a bass comes close but turns away without striking. It might be a tiny water movement around a topwater lure, yet no strike. We might see a twig or a bush move as our bait passes by or a dimple or swirl in the water somewhere around the boat. It could be as primary as a shad jumping even if we don't see the bass chasing it. These are ways the fish tell us what to do, how to fish, and ultimately how to catch 'em.

Prayer, like bass fishing, is a two-way conversation. We need to be aware of what God is telling us as He answers our prayers. Sometimes God immediately performs miracles and gives us a resounding "yes" to our petitions. Sometimes it's a resounding "no." Whether we realize it or not at the time, that "no" will always be God's will—and in our best interest. God's in control. He knows the very best time to answer and will do so when we need it the most.

PRAYER
Lord God, we accept Your perfect will and perfect timing for the answers to our prayers.

GOD'S SPORT
of FISHING

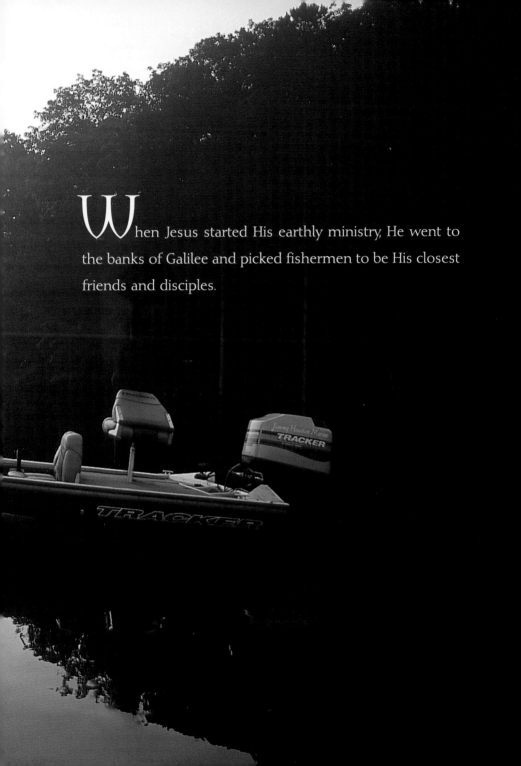

When Jesus started His earthly ministry, He went to the banks of Galilee and picked fishermen to be His closest friends and disciples.

God so loved the world that He gave His only begotten Son, that whoever believes in Him should not perish but have everlasting life.

-JOHN 3:16

One of the keys to becoming a better fisherman is to learn better presentations. The first question most anglers ask others who are catching fish is "What did you catch them on?" While the correct lure is important, the presentation of that lure is equally important.

Keep in mind that presentation is not casting accuracy; presentation deals with depth, speed, and motion. A spinnerbait, for example, can be fished at just about any depth and at a wide variety of speeds. How a fisherman controls the presentation is often the difference between catching fish or not.

One of the most tricky baits in regard to presentation is a suspended jerk bait, such as a Smithwick Rogue or Bomber Long A. First you need to make sure these baits are running perfectly straight in order to get the maximum depth. You do this by making a long cast and reeling the bait back in very fast. If it veers to the left or right, you must adjust it until the bait runs straight.

Once this is done, the fun begins. You wind and jerk the bait down to get it as deep as possible. Then you need to determine what presentation of jerking is best for that day. Usually, a very slight movement of the rod tip (four to six inches) is best. Sometimes, however, the bass want a very severe and fast jerk of the rod. To complicate matters, the length of pause between jerks is also important. Find the proper presentation, and you will catch fish.

Presentation is also key in our daily witness for Christ. But unlike fishing, I don't think we need to be concerned about a myriad of presentations. What we really need to be is *consistent*. We should be spirit-filled in all of our doings, letting folks see Jesus in everything we do.

The gospel of Jesus is straightforward and consistent. It's the same it has always been. Our daily witness to our Savior should be just as straightforward and consistent.

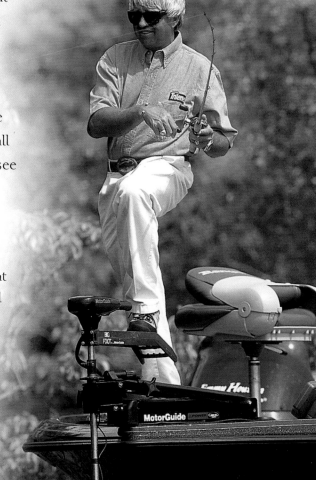

PRAYER

Father, instill in us the desire to present ourselves as faithful and true servants so that others might see the light of Jesus Christ in our lives each day.

RAINY DAYS

> If you confess with your mouth, "Jesus is Lord" and believe in your heart that God raised him from the dead you will be saved.
>
> —ROMANS 10:9 NIV

When the weatherman predicts rain for the weekend, most folks groan. Rain sure can ruin a lot of activities or cause a severe drop in attitude. Rainy days can also be miserable out on the lake, especially if it's cold. It seems like no amount of fancy rain gear can keep you dry and warm when it's pouring. The fact that you're running around the lake in a fast bass boat only complicates the problem.

Amazingly, some of the best bass fishing days are during the rain. Visibility is cut down for the fish, and the low light conditions created by the rain and clouds make a bass less spooky. Additionally, most rain is associated with a frontal passage, which generally produces a rapidly falling barometer. This increases the size of the bass's strike zone and causes him to move to the outside of cover or structure. My rule of thumb when it starts raining is to throw a spinnerbait and run it close to the surface. I believe the bass will be looking up.

We can learn a lesson from this because there are times when telling others of our faith in God isn't successful. Sometimes we find our conviction to witness and our courage challenged. But God places us in situations where He has souls to save. He's equipped us with His Holy Spirit to make our witness work under all conditions. Think

about Jonah, the guy who got caught by the fish. He witnessed under impossible conditions, and the whole city of Nineveh was saved.

When the thunder and lightning abound all around us and the Devil throws up obstacles to a successful witness, just remember: that's when the catch can be the best!

PRAYER

Father, we thank You that even in adversity we feel the strength to stand strong and speak of the wonders that You can perform in all lives.

BLUEBIRD SUNNY DAYS

Jesus said, "I am the resurrection and the life. He who believes in me will live, even though he dies; and whoever lives and believes in me will never die. Do you believe this?

-JOHN 11:25-26 NIV

Golly, do I love the spring! This is when God's magic really comes alive to fishermen. It's what we look forward to all winter.

The key to catching fish on sunny days is water temperature. We're simply looking for the warmest water to fish. This warm water will act like a magnet in drawing fish. I think the magic water temperature is fifty-eight degrees—the temperature where the bass become more active and show up in greater numbers in the shallows. A stable fifty-eight degrees is really what we're looking for, not

fifty-eight degrees at the top of the afternoon, then falling back to fifty degrees at night, which, in fact, can produce some of the worst fishing.

Another key factor is nighttime temperatures. Watch for those nights where it only gets down to fifty-five or sixty degrees. The next day's fishing is going to be great! Make sure you have a good temperature gauge or two on your boat, and get into the habit of watching it closely at all times.

As great as that perfect sun-filled spring day is, think about what God has prepared for us in heaven. The Bible teaches us that we can't even imagine how great heaven will be. And the really super part is that it's not just a magical spring day or two, it's for eternity.

As much as we need the sun to exist here on earth, there's no need for it in heaven. God will provide all the light and warmth we need. We yearn for perfect sunny days, yet God has designed a plan to give us perfect days forever. The plan itself is perfect. All we need to do is believe on Jesus Christ as our Savior, repent of our sins, and turn our lives over to Him. Nothing we can do earns this heaven; it's a gift from God.

PRAYER

Father, we're so thankful for the gift of eternal life. We pray that others who don't know You as we do will yield their lives to Jesus.

FOLLOW THE GUIDE'S ADVICE

Jesus said, "If anyone desires to come after Me, let him deny himself, and take up his cross, and follow Me.

-MATTHEW 16:24

One of the best ways to have a good fishing trip on a strange lake is to hire a guide. Most guides will provide everything you need. They've got the boat, motor, rods, reels, and lures. You can bring your own gear, but usually you just show up.

Additionally, guides have the knowledge and expertise. A guide will help you pick the right lure, show you how to use it, and direct the location of your casts. Also, the guide knows where the fish are. Guides are on the water a lot, and they keep good track of all that's going on. They're familiar with the patterns, what the fish are doing, water temperature, vegetation growth, and so forth. When they stop the boat and tell you to start fishing, you have an above-average chance to catch fish. All you need to do is follow the guide's advice.

We also have a Guide to follow in life. That Guide is God Himself. He is a Guide who always provides everything we need. He gives us every breath we take. He provides our food, clothing, and shelter. He provides our wife or husband. He provides everything we need in our jobs and our career. If we will pray daily and ask Him, He'll give us answers to our most difficult questions and problems.

Our Guide also has all the knowledge, wisdom, understanding, and expertise we need in life. Not only does He have all this information, but He's written it down for us in the Bible. He's ready to share all this life-changing information quicker than any fishing guide will take you to his favorite fishing hole. If you haven't taken advantage of this Guide you're missing out on the greatest "catch" of your life.

PRAYER

Father, lead us, teach us, and guide us in all that we do so that all we accomplish will bring praise and glory to You.

FISHING NOTES